Think Your Way to Wealth Action Plan

The Master Class Series

Awakened Mind

Miracle

The Mastery of Good Luck

The Science of Getting Rich Action Plan

Think Your Way to Wealth Action Plan

The Master Class Series

Think Your Way to Weath Action Plan

A MASTER CLASS COURSE WITH

Mitch Horowitz

MEDIA

MEDIA

Published 2019 by Gildan Media LLC
aka G&D Media
www.GandDmedia.com

FIRST EDITION 2019

Interior design by Meghan Day Healey of Story Horse, LLC

Library of Congress Cataloging-in-Publication Data is available
upon request

ISBN: 978-1-7225-0224-9

10   9   8   7   6   5   4   3   2   1

Contents

Introduction
A Meeting of Giants

As Napoleon Hill described it, this program began as a dialogue he had as a young journalist with steel magnate Andrew Carnegie in 1908. Hill said that he planned to interview Carnegie but instead received a tutorial in the principles behind achieving success—and something more. The industrialist urged his visitor to make an intensive study of the lives of high achievers and notable figures in both history and early twentieth-century life to determine whether they possessed a set of common habits, ideals, and practices.

Hill said he spent twenty years making such a study, which resulted in his 1928 classic *The Law of Success*, his landmark *Think and Grow Rich* in 1937, and finally the book that forms the basis of this program, *Think Your Way to Wealth*, in 1948. The principles that Hill discovered laid the foundation for the field of business motivation as it exists today.

I have never been able to historically verify whether the Hill-Carnegie meeting took place. No contemporaneous article or published interview by Hill exists, and Carnegie made no mention of the fetching young journalist in his autobiography, which appeared in 1920, the year after his death. Hill did not begin referring to the fateful meeting until nearly a decade after Carnegie died.

But nor is such a meeting implausible. In 1908, Hill was writing for *Bob Taylor's Magazine*, a general interest and inspirational journal published by Taylor, the former governor of Tennessee. Hill's author photo and byline appear in a 1908 issue, and the magazine, like many periodicals of the day, featured profiles of business movers-and-shakers, and stories of how they attained their success. An interview with Carnegie would have been the ultimate "get."

Whatever transpired, I have no doubt as a historian, seeker, and longtime reader of Hill's material that he dedicated the twenty years described to his study of the principles of success. Like many of Hill's admirers, I am repeatedly struck by the breadth, richness, and practicality of his material. More so, I can attest from personal experience that *it works*. I often mark 2013 as a turning point in my life: it was the year that I determined to read *Think and Grow Rich* in a more than casual way: I was done with skimming and cherry-picking among his chapters; I vowed to approach every single technique as though my life depended upon it. And, in a sense, it did. Maybe yours does, too. Things began to happen: my career as a writer, speaker, narrator, lecturer, and television presenter flourished.

The program Hill presents in *Think Your Way to Wealth* (which he also published under the title *How to Raise Your Own Salary*) is structured as a dialogue between him and Carnegie. I narrated the program as my first full-length audio book in 2011—yet, in all honesty, I found the original work verbose and artificial-seeming in its dialogue. For Hill, it reflected a rare departure from his usual crisp and to-the-point writing style. This may have reflected deadline pressures. Yet the ideas within the book are absolutely gleaming explorations of hard-won and effective insights in how to actualize your aims in the world. For that reason, this Action Plan distills and emphasizes the most vital and applicable elements of *Think Your Way to Wealth*. Each of these ten lessons captures, updates, and shows how to apply Hill's ideas.

This Action Plan explores some of Hill's most basic ideas, such as the unparalleled importance of possessing a Definite Chief Aim, and carefully considers some of the teacher's more controversial or neglected—but nonetheless vital—insights, such as the question of "sex transmutation" and the existence of "cosmic habit force."

I hope you will find this program a deeply useful introduction or refresher to Hill's success philosophy. It gives me great personal joy to explore with you both Hill's core concepts and those that are too easily bypassed or overlooked, and in a manner that you can begin applying today.

Lesson
ONE

A Definite Chief Aim

I often tell people that if you take only a single idea from the work of Napoleon Hill, make it the cultivation and possession of a Definite Chief Aim. Hill found the concept so important that he capitalized it, as I continue to do here.

This idea opens and informs every chapter of *Think Your Way to Wealth*. There is literally no greater step toward power, success, and achievement than possessing one finely honed, passionately felt, singular aim in life. It can appear difficult to select one overriding aim. Life places many demands on us, from parenting and caregiving to recovery and breadwinning. But it is a law of nature that concentration brings force, just as rays of light focused into a single beam bring searing power. Indeed, it is a tough but transcendent law of life that if you can focus with brilliant clarity on one obsessively felt, emotionally charged aim, you are almost certain to receive what you want or something close to it.

It is also true that a deeply felt aim might require you to downplay certain things in life. This should not include personal health, as will be explored in lesson eight. But it should be kept in mind that a well-selected aim can cover many bases, perhaps allowing you to help loved ones or serve your own needs in ways that you might not have previously imagined. Let's say your aim is wealth. Although money is certainly not the answer to all things in life, it can solve problems, make up for shortages in time, and help bridge distances. Financial resources have their limits but they can answer urgent needs.

An aim must be specific. Merely wanting money is not enough. Everyone, to some greater or lesser degree, wants money. You must have a plain, realistic, and definite way of getting there. Napoleon Hill records Andrew Carnegie telling him:

My own major purpose is that of making and marketing steel. I conceived that purpose while working as a laborer. It became an obsession with me. I took it to bed with me at night, I took it to work with me in the morning. My Defi-

nite Purpose became more than a mere wish; it became my burning desire. That is the only sort of definite purpose that brings results.

I must emphasize the vast difference between a mere wish and a burning desire that has assumed the proportions of an obsession. Everyone wishes for the better things of life but most never go beyond the wishing stage. Men who know exactly what they want of life, however, and are determined to get it, do not stop with wishing. They intensify their wishes into a burning desire and back that desire with continuous effort based on a sound plan.

Making steel may or may not sound like the most romantic goal to you. An aim can be encompassing of nearly anything. But note the simple, definitive clarity of the foregoing passage. These are the ingredients that make an aim possible.

Note, too, the simple realism of the passage. I often tell people that a true aim is actionable. Even if an aim appears far away, you should be able to take some small steps in its direction right away, perhaps seeking out the training or education necessary to approach your goal. If an aim is flat-out fantasy—such as wanting to be an NBA star or an astronaut with no background—it is not an aim at all: it is escapism. An aim, by its definition, is achievable.

A good aim will also rescue you from procrastination, fear (the two are really one and the same), apathy, and all kinds of barriers, for one simple reason: a definite aim is based in the emotions; it is impassioned; its fulfillment feels as important to you as the drawing of breath itself. It is something that you want to pursue more than anything else, including creature comforts, entertainment, and fleeting pleasures. It burns inside you.

Once you have decided on your aim, write it down on a piece of paper—not on your device, but on paper like a contract. It should be succinct, clear, and achievable. Carry this paper with you like your code of life. You needn't share it with anyone. It is your interior compass; your statement of meaning; and your core purpose. If you have chosen it well, and if you act upon it using the means explored in this program, you will get places you never imagined possible. I promise you this because I've personally experienced it. You will, too.

Lesson
TWO

The Emotion of Sex

I am addressing the topic of "sex transmutation" early in this program not only because Hill does so in *Think Your Way to Wealth*, but also because it is one of Hill's most subtle, powerful, and intriguing teachings. The topic of sex energy and success entices and confuses many readers. I want to clarify this alluring yet practicable idea.

In *Think Your Way to Wealth*, Hill quotes Carnegie as saying:

> *The emotion of sex is nature's own source of inspiration through which she gives both men and women the impelling desire to create, build, lead, and direct. Every great artist, every great musician, and every great dramatist gives expression to the emotion of sex transmuted into human endeavor. It is also*

true that men of vision, initiative, and enthu-siasm who lead and excel in industry and business owe their superiority to transmuted sex emotion.

Hill's point is that the urge toward sex-uality is the creative urge of life expressing itself through the individual. This is the urge that drives us to procreate and propagate the species. It is the urge toward coupling and pleasure. It is a vital impulse toward the suste-nance of life. But Hill also teaches—in a manner that squares with a wide range of esoteric spir-itual teachings—that sexuality expresses itself in every act of human creativity, as alluded in the foregoing quote. We are driven not only to propagate life but also to be creative, generative beings in all facets and areas—commercially, artistically, and in matters of health, engineer-ing, trade, communication, travel, culture, and finance. Every time we attempt to actualize our desires, visions, or products in the world, we are, he taught, functioning from this same vital, life-building urge.

Hill writes that once we cultivate this awareness we can actually transmute our sex-ual urge into the development of wealth, art, or anything we wish to establish. The method is simple: when you experience the sexual urge you redirect your thoughts and energies along the lines of a cherished project or piece of work. Through the mental act of redirecting yourself from physical expression to creative expression you harness and place the sexual urge at the back of whatever you are seeking to achieve. This, Hill taught, will add vigor, creativity, and intellectual power to your efforts. This is the act of sexual transmutation.

Hill did not call for celibacy or the sublimation of sexual desire as a physical act. In fact, he underscored the importance of sex not only as a physical release but for therapeutic and stress-reducing purposes. In this regard he was well ahead of his time. But he also noted that at certain moments you could elect to redirect the sexual urge away from physical expression and toward the completion of a cherished task or project. Indeed, Hill said that we're doing this all the time, although unconsciously. The salesperson who possesses personal magnetism, the artist who sees through a project, the entrepreneur who tirelessly builds his or her business—all such people are possessed of powerful sex drives, he taught, and are transmuting these energies toward the accomplishment of their aims. This will harness and elevate your energies and abilities far beyond what you may consider possible.

Lesson
THREE

The Master Mind

Hill quotes Carnegie as saying that he regularly met with a group of trusted advisors, called a Master Mind group: "I met with my Master Mind group nightly, and we entered into a detailed roundtable discussion for the purpose of building plans to carry out the object of my major goal. I heartily recommend this round-table habit."

In plain terms, Hill's conception of a Master Mind group is a support group or fellowship consisting of two or more members (but usually no more than seven to keep things wieldy). The group meets at regular intervals of at least once a week to give support and advice to members on their individual goals. Depending on the nature of the group, members may also offer meditation, prayers, and mental visualization for one another's goals.

At its heart, the Master Mind is a coordinated effort to explore and support one another's plans, purposes, and needs. Hill believed that when several people regularly meet in a spirit of community and mutual support—there can be no divisiveness in the Master Mind—it will level-up the creativity, intuition, and mental faculties of each participant. For this reason, you must select the members of your Master Mind group carefully—the key factors are personal chemistry and cooperation. Divisiveness, political arguments (always keep politics at bay), squabbling, and discursive aims will deplete the functioning of the Master Mind.

I once described *Think and Grow Rich* in a single sentence, which could encompass all of Hill's work: "Emotionalized thought directed toward one passionately held aim—aided by organized planning and the Master Mind—is the root of all accomplishment." This gives you an idea of how central the Master Mind concept is in Hill's system.

"Great power," Hill concluded of the Master Mind, "can be accumulated through no other principle."

The genius—and demand—of Hill's work is that none of his steps are superfluous. Yet in today's digitally removed world it is tempting to skip or ignore this advice. Unless you are already a member of a 12-step or support group, you are probably accustomed to a "go it alone" approach, not wanting to share intimacies with others or to accommodate your already-busy routine to one more meeting. Many of us feel that success is a matter of inner principle and individual effort, and a group meeting seems mawkish or superfluous. I understand those feelings—I struggle with them myself.

But I can personally promise you, as a writer and historian who has studied Hill's methods for years and owes his success to them, and as someone who has been a dedicated member of a Master Mind group since fall of 2013, this step is as vital today as when Hill made the Master Mind the topic of the opening chapter of his first book *The Law of Success* in 1928.

It is characteristic of our cyber age that friends and collaborators not infrequently live and work far distances apart. My own Master Mind group is dispersed from New England to Southern California. We structure things this way: Its four participants, all possessed of supportive natures, good humor, and spiritual values, meet at a regularly designated time by conference call once a week. We begin by reading a short statement of principles, and each participant then individually offers a piece of personal good news from the previous week. Each member then takes a turn describing his wants and needs for the week ahead. After a caller has expressed his wants and needs, each group member suggests advice, ideas, encouragement, and often prayer or other forms of support during off times. The call is generally under one hour.

It is especially important to begin the Master Mind meeting on time, to commence it immediately—eschewing small talk and "meeting chatter"—and to cap the meeting at an hour or less, preferably no more than 45 minutes. (Though this can differ depending on group size.) This is to prevent drifting of attention or resentment when members are pressed for time, or when someone may have greater free time or simply more tolerance for meetings. All of us have enough meetings in life. Most are worthless. The Master Mind, by contrast, is vital and potent; as such, its work should be precise.

This collaborative alliance, if conducted with purpose and harmony, will, in time, yield extraordinary results. I can honestly say that my Master Mind group has proven one of the most helpful and dynamic aspects of each member's life. Our meetings steady me when I am off course, and give me fresh perspective and an added boost to the week. There are also practical benefits, in which economic and business issues are sometimes hashed out. And there is something more at play.

"No two minds," Hill wrote, "ever come together without, thereby, creating a third invisible, intangible force which may be likened to a third mind." This, to him, was the "psychic" phase of the Master Mind, in which the mind may be likened to an energy that is pooled with that of others to intensify intuitions, ideas, and insights. Everyone in a Master Mind group, Hill said, gains heightened insight through the subconscious minds of all the other members. This produces a more vivid imaginative and mental state in which new ideas "flash" into your awareness, he taught.

I can vow to you that, from every perspective, the Master Mind will play an invaluable and practical role in your pursuit of achievement.

Lesson
FOUR

Attractive Personality

Hill wrote often about the traits of an attractive personality, which involve some degree of sex energy as described in a previous lesson, and also an avoidance of boastfulness, intolerance, and general self-centeredness. Rather than review his traits strictly, I want to focus on some personality issues that are particular to our own time.

Many of the personality conflicts that flare up in today's business settings involve emails, texts, and social media postings. Even two decades into the twenty-first century, most people demonstrate little awareness of the dangers of caustic language over digital media. Back in the days of letter writing, business correspondence was crafted with formality. Indeed, a significant degree of standards and etiquette went into most signed letters. Not only has all that gone out the window but the simultaneity of real-time communication and physical remove have so fully disinhibited senders of texts, emails, and postings that sarcasm, anger, eye-rolls, and abruptness have become routine. These things can endanger your relationships and career. If you want to maintain an attractive personality you must go to extra lengths to craft every email or digital communication with decorum and politeness. You will not only avoid needless friction, you will stand out from the herd.

Addiction is also an endangering factor to your personality. Because so many people today telecommute, work from home, or work in informal settings, it is easy and tempting to allow business to mix with intoxication, whether from alcohol or drugs. This isn't a particularly new problem but the temptations are greater precisely because of the artificial remove of digital interaction. I have personally witnessed executives and others communicating in odd ways only to later realize that they were intoxicated. If this happens on just one occasion, peers, supervisors, investors, and coworkers remember it always.

Another issue to watch for in maintaining an attractive personality and sound relationships is to understand the *illusion of privacy.* Nothing that we do today is really private. Texts and social media postings that seem so enticingly private only lull us into a false sense of safety. Not only can such things be hacked, but emails get shared all the time without the sender's knowledge or consent.

Someone I once worked for told employees that you should never write anything in an email that you wouldn't want read out loud in a court of law with you sitting on the witness stand. Likewise, don't take false security from anonymity. People sometimes hurl insults, indulge in gossip, or rundown other people's projects online from behind the sheen of screen names. Not only do I find this detestable for its cowardice, but it is unreliable. A powerful CEO once gravely embarrassed himself when he was caught flaming a competitor's products under a fake name. Anonymity is pierced all the time, and it will be more so in the future. Never say something under a screen name that you'd be unwilling to say in person.

One of the maladies of twenty-first century life—and sooner or later it happens to all of us—is the mistaken hitting of the "reply all" button on an email. We can never exclusively avoid this error, and accepting that is all the more reason to polish your email tone as a matter of insurance.

Face to face, people are generally friendly and reasonably behaved. But behind the keyboard they often feel foolishly liberated from ordinary decorum. Determine *not* to be among those people. Your personal attractiveness will increase as a matter of course.

Lesson
FIVE

Organized Thinking

Think Your Way to Wealth is positive thinking with teeth. In short, you must take concrete and constant steps in the direction of what you wish to be doing.

Now, your wish can be very bold. I was in contact with a man who held a good job in a real estate agency in Washington D.C.; he was in his late thirties and he said he wanted to be a film producer. He asked: "Is this just too far out?" I said to him, so long as you can take reasonable steps in the direction of your wish, it's not too far out.

And I began to communicate with him about things that he could do: there are lots of colleges and universities around D.C. There are lots of artists in and around D.C. He could go to film festivals and focus on short films and documentaries. Find out what local artists are doing. See if he could help them with treatments and with funding. Maybe he can provide micro-funding for certain films. Maybe certain documentaries can be brought to other producers or other people who can provide funding. Maybe he can become both an investor and someone who assists indie filmmakers with treatments and business opportunities— that's what producers do.

There are so many opportunities for exposure. Such opportunities are not always money making, but for documentarians and makers of short films and student film projects, festivals and viewings are the seedlings of other things that are much bigger. Help artists find their way to such venues, I counseled him. And further, know everything there is to know about what young filmmakers and independent filmmakers and artists deal with in the world and in the marketplace today. Take these steps and effectively you are a film producer.

I was trying to get across to my correspondent that if film producing is really your passionate aim, there are organized and concrete plans that can be taken in that direction. It's not too far out. It may not be remunerative at first—or at all. There are lots of artists and entrepreneurs who keep day jobs. I kept a day job, in effect, for many years. You cannot immediately or always wed your dream to paying the rent. But, nonetheless, *movement* is possible. Now, if the man had told me that wanted to be the first astronaut to go to Mars, I would have dismissed that. You'd have to do a lot of convincing to demonstrate that you could do something on Tuesday that would help further that aim. But I can be convinced, and he could be convinced, that he *could* do something on Tuesday that would further him in becoming a film producer. It's absolutely possible.

So, organized thinking and action are a vital part of this program. This is not a program of sitting back and hoping things will happen to you. This is absolutely a program of action. Organized thinking and planning comes up again and again in the book. And I mean organized planning *with a dollar amount attached to* it. Now, one of the things that Hill asks you to do in *Think and Grow Rich*, and it's vitally important, is that once you come up with your definite chief aim—and once you have distilled it into an exquisitely clear sentence that can be committed to paper and that is plain and specific—you must write down a dollar amount that you wish to earn in connection with your aim, the date by which you wish to earn it, and the services you will provide in exchange for this dollar amount. It can be a progressively earned sum. Almost certainly it's not going to come all at once. You can also select a date that is realistically pegged to the future, though not at so distant a point that it's easy to forget.

It is not only necessary and vital to provide a yardstick for oneself, but to understand that the mind, when it's really charged with emotion, functions as a kind of homing device. Almost like the cybernetic device that exists within a heat-seeking missile. It twists and turns, but finally zeroes in on something.

All of this means that you must be able to take real steps, however small and nascent, in the direction of your goal. And you have to have a written statement of your aim. You must plan and you must act. Every day.

Lesson
SIX

Learning from Defeat

"Every negative emotion," Carnegie tells Hill, "can be transmuted into a constructive power and used for the attainment of desirable ends."

This may sound myopic but I absolutely believe that it is true. I have met with setbacks and temporary defeats—and each one has driven me further in the direction of my aim.

When I was writing my first book *Occult America* I agreed to provide a piece of the work-in-progress as an article to a fairly small metaphysical magazine. They gratefully published it—but when the print magazine reached me at home I discovered that the piece, which I felt that I provided them as a favor and which was frankly of a higher quality than their routine, was buried, more or less used as filler, and not featured on the cover.

This was in no way intended as a slight, but I nonetheless felt dejected—as though my work wasn't highly valued in the very place that it should have been. And I had also provided it for free. The episode felt like a failure. Rather than get depressed, I vowed as I held that magazine in my hands at that moment that I would not write for under-appreciative or irrelevant venues again. In the years immediately ahead my byline appeared in places including the *New York Times, Washington Post, Wall Street Journal, Time, Politico*, and other major national media. And my articles were on the same kinds of esoteric topics I had written about up until then. I didn't compromise. That, too, was a victory.

The initial sting of poor recognition drove me to heights that I might not have otherwise reached for. What felt like a setback became a springboard to action. It was, in a sense, a *lucky failure*—from which mature victories grew

This is the attitude that Hill urges toward failure or defeat, which he continually tells the reader to regard as temporary and never as permanent. I agree with this perspective. Persistence is a vital element of success—but not always for the reasons that one supposes. Although there is moral fortitude behind persistence there is another factor, as well. Every statistician and gambler (or ex-gambler) can tell you that runs of luck invariably reverse, for better or worse. This is a natural law. So, if your aim is well selected, any failure or setback you experience is, by its very nature, temporary.

The great mind-body teacher Moshe Feldenkrais (1904–1984) taught that you should be able to write down at least three solutions to any problem, and possibly many more. I advise doing something similar when you experience setback or defeat: write down a series of actual or possible benefits that have emerged from the experience. Maintain your list—add to it as events or new perspectives occur and check off those benefits that time has validated. Your discoveries will surprise you.

I'll give the final word to Carnegie as quoted by Hill:

Defeat should be looked upon in precisely the same manner that one accepts the unpleasant experience of physical pain, for it is obvious that physical pain is nature's way of informing one that something needs attention and correction. Pain, therefore, may be a blessing and not a curse. The same is true of the mental anguish one experiences when overtaken by defeat. While the feeling is unpleasant, it may be nevertheless beneficial because it serves as a signal by which one may be stopped from going in the wrong direction.

Lesson
SEVEN

The Golden Rule Applied

Hill's analysis of the inner dimensions of the Golden Rule is among my favorite of his teachings. I believe that his ideas about the Golden Rule—something that can seem so familiar we rarely consider it—are potentially life changing. Yet in his most popular work, *Think and Grow Rich*, he omits this step. He does explore it extensively in *The Law of Success* and later in *Think Your Way to Wealth*.

I called his interpretation of the Golden Rule "life-changing"—and I meant that. Several years ago I felt personally stuck in my work with creative-mind and visualizing principles. I couldn't quite explain it but something was holding back my efforts to envision higher possibilities for myself and others.

I found the answer to my predicament in Hill's ideas about the hidden power of the Golden Rule. Of course, the precept "do unto others as you would have them do unto you" appears in virtually every religious and ethical teaching, from the Talmud to the Bhagavad Gita. Dubbed the Golden Rule in late-seventeenth century England, this dictum seems so familiar that we're liable to skip past it. But the Golden Rule holds an inner truth that can make all the difference in your life.

Hill relates the Golden Rule to the phenomenon of "autosuggestion," or the suggestions we continually make to ourselves. What you internally repeat about yourself takes root in your subconscious and determines your self-image. But that process is also triggered by what you think about others.

"Your thoughts of others are registered in your subconscious mind through the principle of autosuggestion," Hill writes, "thereby building your own character in exact duplicate." Hence, he continues: "You must 'think of others as you wish them to think of you.' The law upon which the Golden Rule is based begins affecting you, for good or evil, the moment you release a thought."

When we indulge in fantasies of revenge or "score settling"—which I've done more times than I can count during my morning shaves—

we not only shackle ourselves to past wrongs, but also to the wrongs that we would do in exchange. An adjunct to the Golden Rule could be: *We become what we don't forgive.*

Conversely, thoughts of generosity and forgiveness add that "vital something" to your character, Hill writes, "that gives it life and power." Your thoughts about others are the invisible hand that molds your own character. This is why Hill has Carnegie say: "The real benefits of the Golden Rule Applied do not come from those in whose favor it is applied, but they accrue to the one applying the rule."

If you find yourself bumping against limits, reexamine your relationship to the Golden Rule. Its application—as both an inner and outer phenomena—can literally change your perspective on life and on yourself.

Lesson
EIGHT

The Habit of Health

A philosopher once told me: "If you do not give something its proper attention now it will take all of your attention later."

This is a universal truth. But it has particular resonance in matters of health. In the first chapter I made the point that your definite chief aim must be obsessive. On this there can be no compromise. But sound health must be seen as an arterial part of your pursuit of success. Without it, you will lose everything, and sooner than you think.

Many people today have discovered that choosing sobriety, even in the absence of a drinking problem, leads to greater productivity. The reasons are obvious. A voluntary sobriety movement is on the rise in the U.S. as I write these words. A political commentator once observed, "I quit drinking so I could be more successful—and it worked." This simple statement resonated deeply with me. It reached me at a moment in life when it was just what I needed to hear.

You hardly need me to review the benefits of a good diet and exercise. My personal choice in these areas are a high-protein diet and strength training. In this regard, the fitness writer P.D. Managan has inspired me. I also bike almost everywhere, weather permitting, in New York City. (Whether biking is a safe choice so much as a healthy one is open for debate—I strongly advise that you never get on a bike without a helmet, something I still see many of my fellow city-dwellers doing. They are playing with their lives.)

The point is, health as a lifestyle cannot be separated from your aim, whatever it is. This also includes certain mental habits. Chief among them: not complaining. We hear too little today about the fortifying benefits and ethical solidity of abstaining from complaint. If you are reading or listening to this program from the environs of a developed nation you rarely have anything significant to complain about. Lateness of planes, the taste of medicine, problems with the elevator, slowness of restaurant service, the cable being down again—these are problems that would be considered so luxurious across 90 percent of our world that they do not even warrant attention.

I believe that this kind of routine complaining contributes to anxiety, low-grade depression, and ennui, as well as detracts from one's feeling of wellness. Resolve to quit it today.

Lesson
NINE

Inspiration and Self-Discipline

I once heard a basketball coach tell a group of young players that discipline is more important than inspiration. "Some mornings I will feel inspired and some I won't," he said. "Inspiration comes and goes. But if I am disciplined, if I am dedicated to practicing every day, that will always be there."

Napoleon Hill speaks often about the need for both inspiration and discipline in pursuing an aim. As the coach I just quoted points out, the two are different—but I would argue that they come from the same source: enthusiasm. If you have selected the right aim, one that fills you with purpose, drive, and a sense of self-definition, you will possess both the inspiration and self-discipline to progress daily toward your goal.

"You will always move in the direction of the desire which dominates your mind," spiritual teacher Joseph Murphy wrote in 1954.

I once faced a situation where I was completing a very sensitive section of a book I was a writing; this section, which existed of just three to four pages, dealt with some very morally sensitive historical material and required careful handling. I set myself to the task, or the task simply fell to me through the course of my progress, to complete the section during the final night of a family vacation in Cape Cod. The following morning we had to make an hours-long drive back to New York City in summer beach traffic. I will never forget it: after my two children had gone to bed I stayed up almost all night at the kitchen table writing this section. I worked carefully and steadily, stopping at the point of exhaustion around 4 a.m. I got a couple of hours sleep—my kids where then very young and rose early—and I soon got up and prepared for our drive home. Although tired, I was very happy: I had completed a cherished and sensitive task. For me, this was the perfect marriage of both inspiration and self-discipline. Each enabled the other because I was doing exactly the thing that was my perfect self-expression in life. In Vedic tradition this is sometimes called *dharma*.

Inspiration and self-disciple are natural adjuncts. Together they meld into something greater than their sum, which is the topic of our final lesson.

Lesson
TEN

Cosmic Habit Force

In the final chapter of *Think Your Way to Wealth*, Hill departs from the device of using a dialogue between himself and Carnegie and speaks in his own voice describing Cosmic Habit Force. He calls it:

> *the particular application of energy with which nature maintains the existing relationship between the atoms of matter, the stars and planets, the seasons of the year, night and day, sickness and health, life and death, and more important to us right now, it is the medium through which all habits and all human relationships are maintained, the medium through which thought is translated into its physical equivalent.*

Cosmic Habit Force is Hill's application of what is popularly called The Law of Attraction. And he believes that it is a force that arises from the unity of emotion, intellect, and action. In his words,

> *The method by which Cosmic Habit Force converts a positive impulse or mental desire into its physical equivalent is simple. It merely intensifies the desire into a state of mind known as faith, which inspires one to create definite plans for the attainment of whatever is desired, the plans being carried out through whatever natural methods the resourcefulness of the individual can command. Cosmic Habit Force does not undertake to transmute the desires for money directly into bank balances but it does set into motion the mechanism of imagination through which the most easily available means of converting the desire into money is provided in the form of a definite idea, plan, or method of procedure.*
>
> *This force works no miracles, makes no attempt to create something out of nothing, but it does help an individual, nay it forces him to proceed naturally and logically to convert his thoughts into their physical equivalent by using all the natural media available to him which may serve his purpose. The force*

works so quietly that the individual, unless he is of a philosophical trend of mind, does not recognize his relationship to what is happening to him.

On one occasion, an idea will present itself to his mind in a form that he calls a hunch, and it will inspire him with such definite faith that he will begin at once to act upon it. His entire being has been changed from a negative to a positive state of mind with the result that related ideas flow into his mind more freely. The plans he creates are more definite, and his words have more influence with other people.

By this definition, I believe that faith can also be defined as *persistence*. And this unlocks one of the keys to using Cosmic Habit Force. When you work toward a goal or the completion of a project, idea, or piece of art with tireless application you tap and marshal internal resources that you did not realize existed. When you work and work to the point of exhaustion and then rest, when you return to your project you will discover yourself in possession of a freshness of ideas and abilities that go beyond what would be expected from normal physical and mental renewal. This is one of the reasons it is important to take a break from your work *without feeling that you've completed absolutely everything*. Because when you return you will finish your task in a manner that comports with exactly what Hill is describing.

Certain energies disclose themselves only when we refuse personal limits—when we work with persistence, or faith if you chose, that our aim will not be withheld from us. This doesn't mean making demands on others but only on yourself. Within Hill's formula, I think you can find the inner meaning of a somewhat familiar expression, "God helps those who help themselves." If that statement is, in some sense, literally true, Hill's Cosmic Habit Force comes closer than any other line of reasoning to explaining it. It is yours to use—and thrive from.

About the Authors

Napoleon Hill was born in 1883 in Wise County, Virginia. He was employed as a secretary, a reporter for a local newspaper, the manager of a coalmine and a lumberyard, and attended law school, before he began working as a journalist for *Bob Taylor's Magazine*, an inspirational and general-interest journal. In 1908, the job led to his interviewing steel magnate Andrew Carnegie. The encounter, Hill said, changed the course of his life. Carnegie believed success could be distilled into principles that anyone could follow, and urged Hill to interview the greatest industrialists, financiers, and inventors of the era to discover these principles. Hill accepted the challenge, which lasted more than twenty years and formed the building block for *Think and Grow Rich*. Hill dedicated the rest of his life to documenting and refining the principles of success. After a long career as an author, magazine publisher, lecturer, and consultant to business leaders, the motivational pioneer died in 1970 in South Carolina.

Mitch Horowitz is a PEN Award-winning historian and the author of books including *Occult America; One Simple Idea: How Positive Thinking Reshaped Modern Life;* and *The Miracle Club: How Thoughts Become Reality.* A lecturer-in-residence at the University of Philosophical Research in Los Angeles, Mitch introduces and edits G&D Media's line of Condensed Classics and is the author of the Napoleon Hill Success Course series, including *The Miracle of a Definite Chief Aim* and *The Power of the Master Mind.* His other titles in the Master Class Series include: *The Science of Getting Rich Action Plan*; *Miracle: The Ideas of Neville Goddard*; and *Awakened Mind: How Thoughts Create Reality.* Visit him at MitchHorowitz.com.